NEW YORK
THE CITY AT A GLAN(

CU00758784

120 Wall Street
This Buchman & Kahn-designed
an entire block at the epicentre (
district. Completed in 1931, the t
is a fine example of art deco architecture.

Woolworth Building
A pre-WWI embellishment to the New York
skyline, Cass Gilbert's tower earned National
Historic Landmark status in 1966.
See p015

One WTC
Declared one of the world's tallest structures
in 2013, One WTC's height is 1,776 feet, the year
of the American Declaration of Independence.
An observation deck is due to open in 2015.
See p009

8 Spruce Street
At 265m, this 2011 skyscraper was, briefly, the
highest residential building in the city, pipped
by One57 (see p030) in 2013. Designed by Frank
Gehry, it has a wave-like concrete facade.

Brooklyn Bridge
Fly into JFK Airport and no doubt this is how
you'll cross the East River to arrive downtown.
It was designed by John Augustus Roebling,
who died before its completion in 1883.

Manhattan Bridge
Ralph Modjeski and Leon Moisseiff's 1909
crossing now carries seven lanes of traffic
and four subway tracks. It has undergone
$920m of reconstruction work since 1982.

Empire State Building
Architect William Lamb's high-rise (King Kong's
favourite) opened in 1931, and the views from
the 86th-floor observatory are fabulous.
350 Fifth Avenue, T 212 736 3100

INTRODUCTION
THE CHANGING FACE OF THE URBAN SCENE

Why do we love New York? Perhaps it's that incomparable skyline, or the city's irrepressible spirit. Or the fact that it can challenge even the most cosmopolitan urbanite: if you can't do it here, you probably can't do it anywhere. London may claim the mantle of the greatest metropolis in the world, but Gotham got there first.

In the period following the tragedy of the Twin Towers, New York has gradually regained its enthusiasm for the new. Architects have been reshaping the cityscape, particularly in Manhattan's southern half, and creative industries have sprung up in support of homegrown talent and trades; American design, in particular, is being celebrated and promoted once again. The glamour and the glitz are still there, but originality and sustainability are valued just as highly. The prevalence of retailers selling hand-crafted or artisanal goods, and restaurants focused on farm-to-table, even roof-to-table, shows that New Yorkers expect something authentic for their buck. There has never been a better time to shop or eat out in the Big Apple, whatever your taste or your budget.

Artists and hipsters are still migrating to the outer boroughs, to Brooklyn and, increasingly, to Queens, but now that districts like Williamsburg and Park Slope are as expensive – and elitist – as Tribeca or Chelsea, the less well-trodden areas are the more viable options for setting up home or a business. Formerly on the fringes, these neighbourhoods are fast becoming the centres of cool.

ESSENTIAL INFO
FACTS, FIGURES AND USEFUL ADDRESSES

TOURIST OFFICE
Third floor, 810 Seventh Avenue
T 212 484 1200
www.nycgo.com

TRANSPORT
Airport transfer to Manhattan
AirTrains run 24 hours to the subway and
Long Island Rail Road, which links to Penn
Station. The journey takes 50 minutes
www.panynj.gov/airports/jfk-airtrain.html
Car hire
Avis
T 212 593 8396
Car service
Dial 7 Car & Limousine Service
T 212 777 7777
MetroCard
A seven-day Metro and bus pass costs $55
www.mta.info/metrocard
Subway
Trains run 24 hours a day, every day
www.mta.info
Yellow cabs
T 212 639 9675
(for enquiries such as lost property)

EMERGENCY SERVICES
Emergencies
T 911
Police (non-emergency)
T 311
24-hour pharmacy
CVS
630 Lexington Avenue
T 917 369 8688

CONSULATES
British Consulate-General
845 Third Avenue
T 212 745 0200
www.gov.uk/government/world/usa

POSTAL SERVICES
Post office
90 Church Street
T 1 800 275 8777
Shipping
UPS
T 212 680 3118

BOOKS
**Block by Block: Jane Jacobs and
the Future of New York**
(Princeton Architectural Press)
Here is New York by EB White
(Little Bookroom)
Long Island Modernism 1930-1980
by Caroline Rob Zaleski (WW Norton & Co)

WEBSITES
Architecture/Design
www.cooperhewitt.org
Newspaper
www.nytimes.com

EVENTS
Frieze Art Fair
www.friezenewyork.com
ICFF
www.icff.com
NYCxDESIGN
nycxdesign.com

COST OF LIVING
Taxi from JFK Airport to Manhattan
$60
Cappuccino
$3.50
Packet of cigarettes
$12
Daily newspaper
$2.50
Bottle of champagne
$65

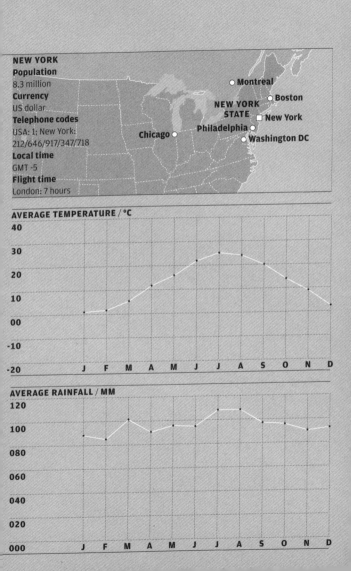

NEW YORK
Population
8.3 million
Currency
US dollar
Telephone codes
USA: 1; New York:
212/646/917/347/718
Local time
GMT -5
Flight time
London: 7 hours

Montreal
Boston
NEW YORK
STATE ☐ New York
Chicago ○ Philadelphia ○
Washington DC

AVERAGE TEMPERATURE / °C

40												
30												
20												
10												
00												
-10												
-20	J	F	M	A	M	J	J	A	S	O	N	D

AVERAGE RAINFALL / MM

120												
100												
080												
060												
040												
020												
000	J	F	M	A	M	J	J	A	S	O	N	D

NEIGHBOURHOODS
THE AREAS YOU NEED TO KNOW AND WHY

To help you navigate the city, we've chosen the most interesting districts (see below and the map inside the back cover) and colour-coded our featured venues, according to their location; those venues that are outside these areas are not coloured.

TRIBECA/THE BATTERY
Manhattan's southern tip could not be more diverse. Downtown's most compelling area, Ground Zero (see p010), is still under construction more than a decade after 9/11. Tribeca is a younger version of Soho, full of design studios (see p074) and refined restaurants such as Atera (see p050).

UPPER WEST SIDE
Archetypal liberal intellectual territory, this residential district benefits from old and new money. The vast Central Park West apartment blocks are like ocean liners steaming through Manhattan. Its cultural focal point is Lincoln Center (see p066), which was recently renovated.

WEST VILLAGE
Darling of both indie and luxury brands (especially along Bleecker Street), the leafy West Village has a vibrant yet intimate ambience. Here, Manhattan assumes a human scale, with cosy neighbourhood eateries, 19th-century townhouses and pretty streets, such as Perry and Charles.

SOHO
Once an artists' quarter, where cast-iron industrial buildings were turned into lofts and studios, the mood is now more Kenzo than De Kooning, and Soho can feel very touristy. However, it does have great shops such as The Apartment (see p034), Proenza Schouler (see p076) and Alexander Wang (see p087), and good galleries (see p036).

UPPER EAST SIDE
This is quintessential rich-bitch New York, replete with liveried doormen helping social X-rays carry bag upon bag after a day's shopping on Madison. It's also home to the city's venerable museums: the Met (see p064), Guggenheim (T 212 423 3500) and Cooper-Hewitt (T 212 849 8400).

MIDTOWN
NYC's central business district includes Times Square – the backdrop for the bright lights of Broadway or a tacky, neon-lit, tourist hell, depending on your take. Highlights include the Museum of Arts and Design (T 212 299 7777) and rooftop bar at the Viceroy hotel (see p016).

CHELSEA
The unmissable attraction in Chelsea is the High Line (see p037); the area is also a locus of heavyweight art galleries. Stylish venues like Hôtel Americano (see p026) and The Monarch Room (see p042) have helped to restore a hipness to the quarter that gentrification had diminished.

EAST VILLAGE/LOWER EAST SIDE
Traditionally a working-class, immigrant area, the Lower East Side is still a cultural melting pot, and home to some of NYC's edgier art spaces and bars, as well as SANAA's New Museum (see p065). To the north, the East Village has been heading upmarket since the 1980s, while Noho draws fashionistas to its trendy boutiques.

LANDMARKS

THE SHAPE OF THE CITY SKYLINE

How can you pick out a landmark building in a city that possibly contains more instantly recognisable skyscrapers than any other? Perhaps owing to its relative youth, New York has never been shy about making a statement with modern architecture. And thanks to the affluence of many of its citizens, the Big Apple has been able to call on the talents of almost every architect of note over the past 100 or so years, to create its incomparable skyline.

Following the 2014 opening of Davis Brody Bond's subterranean National September 11 Memorial Museum (Liberty Street, T 212 312 8800), accessed via Snøhetta's glass pavilion, the new World Trade Center site is gradually moving towards completion. At its heart lies Michael Arad and PWP's plaza (overleaf), where two massive waterfalls are positioned in the footprints of the Twin Towers. Rearing above this, two of the site's five main towers are complete: the 541m One WTC (285 Fulton Street), by SOM's David Childs, which is the tallest building in the western hemisphere (with spire); and Fumihiko Maki's quietly impressive 298m 4 WTC (Greenwich Street). Although Santiago Calatrava's transportation hub is still under construction, a significant portion of the site is finally accessible to the public. Funding issues and changes to the original design have caused delays to Frank Gehry's performing arts centre, but work is still scheduled to start in 2016.

For full addresses, see Resources.

9/11 Memorial
Achieving consensus on an appropriate
memorial for the victims of 9/11 was
never going to be easy, and hundreds
of ideas were debated. Architect Michael
Arad's winning concept, 'Reflecting
Absence', is boldly minimal: two dramatic
granite pools, each with a central void,
are inscribed around the edge with the
2,983 names of those who perished.
Albany Street/Greenwich Street

AT&T Building

This massive 1932 art deco structure, designed by American architect Ralph Walker, was originally known as the AT&T Long Distance Building; it housed the telecommunications giant's transatlantic offices and equipment. In the 1990s, the company made this its HQ, although AT&T has since sold up. Its brick-clad bulk (all 106,838 sq m of it) is quintessentially Gotham-like in form, and the lobby boasts the obligatory tiled map of the world on one wall. The building may not be among the city's best-known landmarks, nor even Walker's finest work (this is usually said to be the erstwhile Irving Trust Company headquarters at 1 Wall Street). However, from its profile to the materials used, the AT&T could not be found anywhere except New York, and for that it is a masterwork.
32 Sixth Avenue, www.32sixthave.com

Hearst Tower

Fresh from remodelling London's skyline with 30 St Mary Axe (the Gherkin), Norman Foster tackled the HQ of the Hearst media empire. The diamond-faceted facade of this 46-storey tower, completed in 2006, thrusts out of an existing art deco building that was commissioned in the 1920s by media mogul William Randolph Hearst; the six-storey structure was always intended to form the base of a landmark high-rise.

The new blends seamlessly with the old, thanks to the dramatic lobby that extends up through the lower floors to provide access to all parts of the building. And it's not just a pretty sight. The tower is environmentally friendly too – it was constructed with 90 per cent recycled steel and consumes about 25 per cent less energy than its neighbours.
300 W 57th Street

Austrian Cultural Forum

In a city where bigger is often thought to be better, Austrian Raimund Abraham created a diminutive wonder in 2002 with his first major US project, although he had lived in New York for more than 30 years. 'My intention was to resolve the extreme condition of the smallness of the site,' he said. The architect, who died in 2010, succeeded. The Cultural Forum is a brilliant design: a glass-skinned sliver, a mere 7.6m wide, rising to 85m. Its presence belies its dimensions, and the ACFNY's brooding facade – reminiscent, in profile, of an Easter Island statue – outshines all the surrounding buildings. When it was unveiled, it was hailed by many as the most important structure to have been erected in Manhattan in four decades. *11 E 52nd Street, T 212 319 5300, www.acfny.org*

Woolworth Building

For some 17 years after its opening in 1913, Cass Gilbert's Woolworth Building was the tallest in the world. His client, five-and-dime-store magnate Frank W Woolworth, was wealthy enough to pay the $13.5m price tag in cash. This, coupled with the structure's gothic proportions, earned it the moniker 'the cathedral of commerce'. Even today, the sheer scale of the building is awe-inspiring: it stands at 241.4m high, and there's room for 14,000 office workers across 54 floors, all of which are served by 30 elevators. The top 30 floors are currently being converted into a handful of apartments. In the spectacular lobby, which is lined with marble and lavishly decorated with mosaics and bronze, there are medieval-style gargoyles, including caricatures of Woolworth and Gilbert.
233 Broadway

HOTELS
WHERE TO STAY AND WHICH ROOMS TO BOOK

The boutique hotel scene is resurgent in NYC, and gone are the days when staying in Midtown meant forgoing all things stylish. Now, it is the place to be, as the Roman and Williams-designed Viceroy (124 W 57th Street, T 212 830 8000), the business-oriented Quin (101 W 57th Street, T 212 245 7846) and the towering Park Hyatt (see p030) all hold court on 57th Street, close to Central Park. This revival has also prompted established hotels to up their game, among them the Loews Regency (540 Park Avenue, T 212 759 4100), which underwent a $100m makeover in 2014.

Downtown, hotelier Sean MacPherson, of The Jane (113 Jane Street, T 212 924 6700) and The Bowery (335 Bowery, T 212 505 9100), is behind two 2014 launches: The Marlton (see p018) in Greenwich Village, and the 184-room Ludlow (180 Ludlow Street, T 212 432 1818), whose oak-panelled rooms and mosaicked floors pay tribute to the heritage of the Lower East Side.

There are plenty of attractive options on the West Side too. A few blocks from the Hudson River, Hotel Hugo (525 Greenwich Street, T 888 335 8944) mixes raw industrial elements with glossy finishes and vertical gardens. In Chelsea, The High Line Hotel (180 Tenth Avenue, T 212 929 3888), in the former General Theological Seminary, which dates to the mid-19th century, cuts a dash amid the neighbourhood's cluster of contemporary art galleries.

For full addresses and room rates, see Resources.

The Broome

Despite an overhaul lasting seven years, this five-storey, 14-room boutique hotel, which once housed artists' lofts and is now owned by four Frenchmen, is faithful to its origins. Art from the owners' private collections adorns the walls and the serene atrium (above) provides guests with some reprieve from the bustle of Soho beyond. All the rooms are tastefully done out in Mitchell Gold + Bob Williams furnishings, and overlook Broome Street or the inner courtyard. The home-from-home feel is enhanced by thoughtful touches such as the complimentary morning pastries from nearby bakery Ceci Cela (T 212 274 9179). We recommend booking the one-bedroom Penthouse, which has a roof terrace and panoramic views of the neighbourhood. *431 Broome Street, T 212 431 2929, www.thebroomenyc.com*

The Marlton

Hotelier Sean MacPherson once described this luxe bijou hotel as 'Honey, I shrunk the Ritz'. Nestled in the heart of Greenwich Village, the former college dorm has been transformed into a nine-storey tribute to Parisian chic. Sculpted mouldings and Serge Mouille-style ceiling lamps bedeck the petite but light-filled guest rooms, such as the Queen Deluxe (above), while the lobby features patterned carpets, darkwood panels and reupholstered sofas. The hotel also houses an elegant brasserie, Margaux (T 212 321 0111); Bellocq tea and organic Ferndell coffee can be ordered in the Espresso Bar (opposite). It's all a wonderfully polished counterpoint to the urban-industrial aesthetic that has proliferated the city in recent years.
5 W 8th Street, T 212 321 0100, www.marltonhotel.com

Wythe Hotel
Opened in 2012, the Wythe has given
Brooklyn the grown-up hotel it deserves.
The factory building has been wisely
preserved, and the decor of reclaimed
pine furniture and bespoke wallpaper
(King Room, pictured) is the right foil,
softening the industrial edge. Dine at
Reynard (T 718 460 8004), then drink
in the Manhattan skyline from the bar.
80 Wythe Avenue, T 718 460 8000

Four Seasons

It's the Four Seasons, so of course it is impeccable. Perhaps the Canadian group's crown jewel, the IM Pei-designed tower is still said to be one of the city's tallest hotels, and by golly does the Chinese-born architect give good power lobby. The service is exemplary, and although not all the rooms are to our taste, they are large and luxurious; the 400 sq m Ty Warner Penthouse (above) is stunning (and pricey, being one of the world's most expensive hotel suites). At a pinch, we think the views looking north over Central Park are the best, but the southern aspect is pretty impressive too. Cap off your day in an oversized chair by the fireplace in the Ty Lounge, with a perfect martini and some fascinating people-watching.
57 E 57th Street, T 212 758 5700, www.fourseasons.com/newyork

The Chatwal

This 1905 building was originally designed by architect Stanford White. In 2010, it was renovated by Thierry Despont, who applied his own updated version of art deco in dazzling fashion. The 76 guest rooms, including the grand Producer Suite (above), are decorated with vintage 'steamer trunk' wardrobes, fine suede walls and old subway signs. Off the lobby, in The Lambs Club restaurant (T 212 997 5262), Geoffrey Zakarian continues to rate highly with his modern American cuisine. The 18th-century French stone fireplace, red-leather banquettes and warm lighting make a handsome backdrop for the equally alluring food, which pairs like a charm with a cocktail list conceived by NYC nightlife veteran Sasha Petraske. *130 W 44th Street, T 212 764 6200, www.thechatwalny.com*

Andaz Wall Street

Wall Street seems like a logical location for a full-service, luxury hotel, but previous efforts have either fallen short or failed outright. The Andaz, designed by David Rockwell, is Hyatt's attempt, making the most of a prime position and learning from its predecessors' missteps. Housed in a former Barclays Bank building, dating to 1982, the hotel's standard lobby and check-in desk have been replaced by a lounge with an iPad-wielding host. The 253 rooms are large and well proportioned. We opted for Room 1513 (above), looking on to Wall Street; those facing south-west overlook Hanover Square. The cuisine in Wall & Water (T 212 699 1700), the Andaz's mod-American restaurant, is tasty, so you will be grateful for the lower-level gym. *75 Wall Street, T 212 590 1234, www.andaz.com*

Crosby Street Hotel

Although it's right in the heart of the city, Crosby Street is one of those New York thoroughfares that still feels off the radar. Rising 11 storeys above a former parking lot, the red-brick Crosby Street Hotel (the only American outpost for Britain's Firmdale Hotels group) feels old New York outside, new New York inside. In the lobby, which has full-height windows, Kit Kemp introduced colourful paintings and fabrics, and a monumental steel skull sculpture by Jaume Plensa. Vintage dressmaker's mannequins and oversized headboards set a quirky tone in the 86 rooms, which look towards Soho; opt for a One Bedroom Suite (above). Belly up to The Crosby Bar, decorated in an eclectic style, for a well-crafted cocktail or afternoon tea.
79 Crosby Street, T 212 226 6400, www.firmdalehotels.com

Hôtel Americano

Tucked within Chelsea's gallery district, Grupo Habita's debut American hotel is a class act, from architect Enrique Norten's mesh-covered exterior right through to the sleek interiors by Parisian designer Arnaud Montigny. The 56 rooms exude urban cool, thanks to low platform beds and midcentury modern furnishings in a palette of black, grey and yellow; the ninth-floor Studio Suite (above) is among the best. The rooftop lounge, La Piscine (T 212 525 0000), serves crisp cocktails and has knockout views of the High Line (see p037); downstairs, in The Americano (T 212 525 0000), chef Joseph Buenconsejo cooks up zippy French cuisine with a Latin edge. The vibe is laidback but full of brio, especially during Sunday brunch.
518 W 27th Street, T 212 216 0000, www.hotel-americano.com

The Nolitan

Design firm Grzywinski+Pons were faced with the challenge of creating a sense of community within a community for the Nolita area's first boutique hotel. The result is an industrial-chic low-rise that blends in adeptly with its surroundings. There are 57 snug rooms, comprising oak flooring, concrete ceilings, Corian accents and floor-to-ceiling windows; some have private balconies. The public spaces are generous: there's a sizeable roof terrace and, on the ground level, the lobby (above) connects to a library and a café. The many amenities (such as bikes and skateboards) are varied enough to attract trendsetters as well as business travellers, and despite residing on a traffic-heavy street corner, the hotel maintains a tranquil ambience. *30 Kenmare Street, T 212 925 2555, www.nolitanhotel.com*

The Standard East Village

Rebranding an existing hotel is no easy task, but André Balazs was equal to the challenge. Since acquiring the Cooper Square Hotel in 2012, he has steadily given it The Standard treatment, while still receiving guests. Designed in part by Shawn Hausman, it now has 145 rooms (Noho Studio, pictured), and is a relaxed alternative to its High Line cousin.
25 Cooper Square, T 212 475 5700

Park Hyatt

Plenty of effort has gone into creating a memorable setting for the Park Hyatt's first New York property, now the group's global flagship. Spread over 25 floors of Christian de Portzamparc's striking 79-storey tower, One57, the 2014 hotel is all about luxury, from the modern chandeliers in the ballroom to the metal screens and lacquered minibars in the guest rooms, designed by Yabu Pushelberg. Boasting floor-to-ceiling windows, the rooms are said to be the largest in New York, with the standard options (above) starting at 44 sq m. Bathrooms are stocked with Le Labo products, but don't let that stop you visiting the three-storey Spa Nalai, which has an indoor swimming pool that affords stunning views over mid-Manhattan.

153 W 57th Street, T 646 774 1234,
www.newyork.park.hyatt.com

The NoMad Hotel

Injecting a shot of lavishness into Midtown, The NoMad marries old-world charm with New York sophistication in a turn-of-the-century Beaux Arts building. Attention to historical detail characterises Jacques Garcia's treatment of the 168 rooms and public areas, such as the lobby (above). Vintage Heriz rugs cover a salvaged maple wood floor, and the library's 200-year-old spiral staircase was imported from France.

Reserve one of the lofty Grande Rooms, or a Suite for a diverting street vista. The restaurant, NoMad (T 347 472 5660), is helmed by Will Guidara and Daniel Humm of Michelin-starred Eleven Madison Park (T 212 889 0905). Fashion label Maison Kitsuné opened its first American boutique adjacent to the hotel (T 212 481 6010). *1170 Broadway, T 212 796 1500, www.thenomadhotel.com*

24 HOURS

SEE THE BEST OF THE CITY IN JUST ONE DAY

You'll never want for things to do in New York. What with all the eating, drinking and shopping, it can be hard to find time for other pursuits, so our recommended plan of attack is to hone in on the cultural highlights of just a few neighbourhoods.

The best way to see the city is on foot, and our itinerary focuses on lower Manhattan. First, grab a coffee at Ninth Street Espresso (75 Ninth Avenue, T 212 652 2100), inside Chelsea Market, before touring the district's numerous galleries, such as David Zwirner (opposite). From here, make for Soho, the former artists' enclave in the heart of downtown, for a dose of retail therapy (see p034). Then refuel with a seafood-focused spread at Navy (137 Sullivan Street, T 212 533 1137). Ease any post-lunch lethargy by following a stroll through the area with a look around Donald Judd's former studio (see p036), before looping back to Chelsea to visit the High Line (see p037) and, when it opens in 2015, Renzo Piano's Whitney Museum (Gansevoort Street/Washington Street, T 212 570 3600).

For dinner, reserve a table at All'Onda (see p038), where the fusion of Japanese and Venetian cuisine has proved a surprising success. Finish proceedings in the East Village: The Toucan & The Lion (342 E 6th Street, T 212 375 8989) and the nearby Death + Company (433 E 6th Street, T 212 388 0882) both have an excellent list of knockout cocktails with some adventurous twists.
For full addresses, see Resources.

10.00 David Zwirner

Representing more than 40 artists, such as Yayoi Kusama, Doug Wheeler and Dan Flavin, and eight artists' estates, David Zwirner now has two galleries in Chelsea. The 19th Street location (T 212 727 2070) occupies three single-storey units that were once garages and stables, while the newer 20th Street gallery (above), opened in 2013, is a LEED-certified new-build by Selldorf Architects. The industrial edge of the exposed concrete facade is tempered by teak window frames and panelling at the entrance. There are two exhibition areas, including a 465 sq m column-free space. While you're in the area, also check out Hauser & Wirth (T 212 790 3900) and Gagosian's galleries on 21st Street (T 212 741 1717) and 24th Street (T 212 741 1111). *537 W 20th Street, T 212 517 8677, www.davidzwirner.com*

12.00 The Apartment by The Line

Opened by über-stylists Vanessa Traina and Morgan Wendleborn, The Apartment is an inviting concept store and physical iteration of the duo's online fashion and lifestyle portal, The Line. Situated in a Soho loft, the showroom is divided into several rooms, each offering an evocative vision of stylish city living. The light-filled interiors are the work of Carl Sprague, a set designer and Wes Anderson collaborator. On display are wares that span the realms of fashion, beauty and design, with items from industry figures such as JW Anderson, Mansur Gavriel, Protagonist, Rodin and ME SkinLab, alongside Jean Prouvé chairs and other vintage curios sourced from local dealers. The studio is open on Wednesdays and Saturdays from about midday, or on other days by appointment.

Third floor, 76 Greene Street,
T 646 678 4908, www.theline.com

13.00 101 Spring Street

Providing a brilliant insight into the life and work of Donald Judd, this former Soho textile factory, which the artist turned into a live/work space in 1968, is now a celebration of his philosophies on art and architecture. Restored by Judd himself, 101 Spring Street came under the wing of the National Trust for Historic Preservation after his death in 1994. A juxtaposition of industrial 19th-century fixtures and Judd's abstract works, the five-storey space also displays furniture and art that Judd collected on his travels or from his peers – other seminal artists of the 20th century, such as Dan Flavin. To gain access to the building, visitors must book one of three daily 90-minute guided tours. Closed on Monday, Wednesday and Sunday.

101 Spring Street, T 212 219 2747, www.juddfoundation.org

15.00 High Line

A strip of elevated parkway on Manhattan's West Side has been the regeneration project on everyone's lips for the past few years. This abandoned 1930s rail track was threatened with demolition in the late 1990s, prompting two local residents, Robert Hammond and Joshua David, to form a non-profit group, Friends of the High Line, to save it. The result, designed by architects Diller Scofidio + Renfro, and James Corner Field Operations, is an inspired public space, used from dawn till dusk. The first section, Gansevoort Street to W 20th Street, opened in 2009, and a second section, to W 30th Street, in 2011. Its final phase, the High Line at the Rail Yards, will run to W 34th Street, wrapping around Hudson Yards (see p064) and opening in three stages from 2014.
T 212 206 9922, www.thehighline.org

20.00 All'Onda

Contributing to the recent renaissance of Greenwich Village, All'Onda takes a fresh look at Venetian fare. Chef Chris Jaeckle's interpretation of *cicchetti*, such as squid-ink or red-squash *arancini*, plus crudo, risotto and pasta, are all served over two levels. The mix of brick walls, tiles, walnut and metallic details is the work of Silvia Zofio and Jack Dakin.
22 E 13th Street, T 212 231 2236

URBAN LIFE

CAFÉS, RESTAURANTS, BARS AND NIGHTCLUBS

Despite the hectic pace of metropolitan life, eating and drinking out are sacred pastimes for New Yorkers. And the diversity of the culinary scene is one of the city's great strengths. Recently, chefs such as John Fraser (see p044) and Daisuke Nakazawa (see p058) have been concentrating on traditional techniques, and rotisserie cooking has also returned to favour; try Narcissa (see p044) or Rotisserie Georgette (14 E 60th Street, T 212 390 8060). Breaking new ground, Nolita's Uncle Boons (7 Spring Street, T 646 370 6650) draws crowds for its offbeat approach to Thai food. Bridging the gap between old and new in Chelsea, chef David Pasternack gives Italian seafood a fresh interpretation at Barchetta (461 W 23rd Street, T 212 255 7400). To the north, in Hell's Kitchen, Ivan Ramen Slurp Shop (T 212 582 7942) in Gotham West Market (600 Eleventh Avenue, T 212 582 7940) is ideal for a quick lunch.

Brooklyn affords Manhattanites plenty of reasons to venture away from the island. The Elm (160 N 12th Street, T 718 218 1088) in Williamsburg serves inventive French cuisine and has a stellar wine list. Meanwhile, Greenpoint has been garnering attention, thanks to venues such as Tørst (opposite). There is still plenty of hipster irony in the borough too. At Royal Palms Shuffleboard Club (514 Union Street, T 347 223 4410) in Gowanus, try your hand at the retirees' sport spurred on by some food-truck fare and cocktails. *For full addresses, see Resources.*

Tørst

Since its 2013 launch, Tørst has taken the pairing of food and craft beer to another level, and that's all down to the skills and imagination of the venue's owners, Daniel Burns (ex-Noma and Momofuku) and Jeppe Jarnit-Bjergsø (Evil Twin brewery). An alternating selection of 21 beers is available on tap, and there are more than 200 bottles to choose from; we kicked off with an Evil Twin and a Tørst exclusive from the Swedish brewery Omnipollo. The bar snacks have a Danish slant (rye bread, smoked trout, cured meats) and the Scandi theme extends to the interiors. Brooklyn designers hOmE accented the space with a combination of woods and marble. If the beer-drinking works up your appetite, try Luksus, adjoined to the bar.
615 Manhattan Avenue, T 718 389 6034, www.torstnyc.com

The Monarch Room
The dark wood, raw concrete and poured-in-place staircase all reference the industrial roots of this Chelsea restaurant, a former warehouse. Lending the interior their trademark mod-vintage touch, Roman and Williams installed a 6m-long mahogany bar and leather banquettes: a stylish setting for Michael Citarella's finely honed American menu.
408 W 15th Street, T 646 790 7070

Narcissa

In The Standard East Village (see p028), Narcissa has gained quite the following since its launch in 2014. The restaurant uses produce grown on André Balazs' farm, Locusts on Hudson, and has built a reputation for its rotisserie cooking and a West Coast-style approach to flavours and ingredients. Chef John Fraser, who's also behind the Upper West Side's Dovetail (T 212 362 3800), applies the method to meat and poultry, in dishes such as roast baby chicken with spiced sausage and truffle broth; and vegetables, like crisped beets with apple and creamed horseradish. The dining room has a cool, Nordic-Shaker edge, with blondwood accents and a mural (opposite) by artist Andrew Kuo. Booking well in advance is a must.
21 Cooper Square, T 212 228 3344, www.narcissarestaurant.com

Runner & Stone

Bread is still having a moment in New York, courtesy of a group of artisan bakers raising the profile of the humble loaf. At Runner & Stone in Gowanus, owners Chris Pizzulli, formerly of Blue Ribbon (T 212 274 0404), and Peter Endriss, of Bouchon Bakery (T 212 823 9366) and Per Se (T 212 823 9335), focus on all things baked. Call in for breakfast and order a baguette, plain or buckwheat, served with freshly churned butter – great on its own, but even better accompanied by a mug of Crop to Cup coffee. For the interior, Manhattan architects Latent Productions repurposed hundreds of flour sacks to line the walls in a brick-like formation, and Withers & Grain salvaged wood from Brooklyn water towers to construct the tables and chairs. *285 3rd Avenue, T 718 576 3360, www.runnerandstone.com*

Potlikker

Reimagined comfort food is the speciality at chef Liza Queen's popular restaurant on Williamsburg's south side. Rather than following a singular culinary tradition, Queen, who headed over to Vietnam for ideas after closing her first venture, The Queen's Hideaway, concentrates on unexpected flavour combinations. One highly addictive dish is her Dutch pancake, wonderfully light and smothered in goat's cheese, homemade hot-pepper jelly, crispy bacon and fried oysters. Queen's sister, interior designer Samantha Crasco (who decorated The Greenwich Hotel's guest rooms), broke away from the ubiquitous ramshackle Brooklyn aesthetic, lending Potlikker a clean-lined, cheerful air. The curved wooden bar is particularly cool. *338 Bedford Avenue, T 718 388 9808, www.potlikkerbrooklyn.com*

Pearl & Ash

Chef Richard Kuo oversees the tiny kitchen at the dinner-only Pearl & Ash, serving up small plates with big flavours from around the world. At the bar, sommelier Patrick Cappiello (formerly of Gilt) has compiled one of the most interesting wine lists in the city, and Eben Klemm's cocktails, also designed to complement the food, are similarly inventive; try a Teenage Jesus with manzanilla sherry, pressed pineapple, white ale and orgeat syrup. Brooklyn's Sway Design Collective conceived the interiors, installing poplar tables against an eye-catching wall of shelving filled with moss and ephemera. Hovering between Noho and the East Village, the restaurant is inside The Bowery House, a boutique hostel with 200 'cabin' rooms plus dorms. *220 Bowery, T 212 837 2370, www.pearlandash.com*

Atera

It's all about the journey at Matthew Lightner's acclaimed 18-seat temple to the tasting menu. First, finding Atera can be tricky, as it's located in an unmarked commercial building. Once you're here, a three-hour gastronomic adventure begins. The 20-course menu is revised regularly, but Lightner's technical prowess and visual imagination are present in every morsel, from the starters (mini lobster rolls in a toasted yeast meringue) to the desserts (yogurt with marshmallow and brown butter). Design firm Parts and Labor used reclaimed wood and slate for the interior, softening the look with a vertical garden on the back wall. If you can't get a table, try The Lounge downstairs, which serves cocktails and Lightner's bar snacks.
77 Worth Street, T 212 226 1444, www.ateranyc.com

Wallflower

You could walk right past Wallflower, a discreet West Village bar/restaurant hidden behind window blinds. Beyond the unpretentious guise lies a glorious cocktail bar serving killer drinks. Xavier Herit, who previously tended the bars at ECC and Daniel, has devised a list that makes the most of seasonal ingredients. Expect tipples such as The Dude, which pairs cognac with cold-brewed coffee, port, cream, Angostura bitters, sugar syrup and an egg. On any given night, you'll find the place buzzing with well-heeled locals, ensconced in the booths or cosied up to the panelled bar. The food menu has been designed to complement the drinks: for snacking, order a selection of small plates; for a more substantial meal, there's a prix-fixe menu and a tip-top wine list. *235 W 12th Street, www.wallflowernyc.com*

Alder

Still humming more than a year on, Alder is helmed by the molecular gastronomy pioneer Wylie Dufresne, who has composed a menu of whimsically deconstructed classics. Jennifer Carpenter's interior design matches the inventive mood of the cooking: a textured brick wall is offset by a ceiling of salvaged fencing, hung at varying angles to create a ripple effect.
157 Second Avenue, T 212 539 1900

Antica Pesa

The first outpost of the renowned Roman restaurant, opened in 1922, serves *cucina rustica* in a refined setting, bringing a refreshing urbanity to Williamsburg and its dining scene. The interior designers, Brooklyn-based BArC Studio, created three distinct zones: the front area caters to larger groups; the middle section has a marble bar and snug lounge with a fireplace; and to the rear is the main dining room, decorated with walnut wood, white walls and pendant lights. Order one or two of the pastas, which are superb. *Schiaffoni all'amatriciana* (with cured pork jowl, crushed tomatoes and pecorino) and *tagliolini cacio e pepe* (with parmesan, pecorino and black pepper) are brilliantly executed versions of the Roman classics. *115 Berry Street, T 347 763 2635, www.anticapesa.com*

Momofuku Ssäm Bar

Korean-American David Chang seemingly came out of nowhere to establish himself as one of New York's most exciting chefs. His cluster of restaurants includes the Midtown Má Pêche (T 212 757 5878) and a trio of East Village venues, among them Momofuku Ssäm Bar. Injecting vigour into the now familiar pan-Asian genre, Chang celebrates the colours, flavours and textures of the orient, with some unexpected flourishes. Long, narrow and sleek, with stools and communal tables, MSB doesn't take bookings, but queueing is worth the wait. You can reserve if you're having one of the sharing dishes however, such as the Bo Ssäm: a whole slow-cooked pork shoulder served with white rice, bibb lettuce, kimchi and a dozen oysters.
207 Second Avenue, T 212 254 3500, www.momofuku.com

Toro

Housed within a former Nabisco factory facing the Hudson River, Toro is a laidback affair serving traditional and new-wave Barcelona-style tapas and pintxos. The wood and exposed-brick interiors, by New World Design Builders, draw on the edifice's industrial origins, and large windows allow light to pour into the whole space. Launched by chefs Jamie Bissonnette and Ken Oringer as a Big Apple counterpart to their respected Boston restaurant, Toro seats 125 diners. Grab a stool at the plancha bar to watch the chefs assemble dishes such as grilled corn with aioli, lime, espelette and aged cheese, or roasted bone marrow with beef-cheek marmalade. Wash everything down with some house sangria, whose ingredients change seasonally.
85 Tenth Avenue, T 212 691 2360, www.toro-nyc.com

Sushi Nakazawa

There has been a lot of talk surrounding this Japanese restaurant, headed by chef Daisuke Nakazawa, a long-time apprentice of sushi master Jiro Ono. All the hype is deserved. The *omakase* menu, served at the bar, comes in at a relatively affordable $150 for 20 courses; the menu for guests in the dining room is a little less expensive at $120. Most importantly, the sushi itself is exemplary. Nakazawa presents each course as a single piece of sushi, which allows the focus to remain on each flavour. Top-quality ingredients are flown in from all over the world, including rice imported from his native Japan. It all makes for quite an exquisite experience, about two hours long. The finale will typically involve a lighter-than-air egg custard.

23 Commerce Street, T 212 924 2212,
www.sushinakazawa.com

The Third Man

This Alphabet City cocktail den is the brainchild of chefs Eduard Frauneder and Wolfgang Ban of nearby Edi & The Wolf (T 212 598 1040) and the Michelin-starred Seäsonal (T 212 957 5550) in Midtown. An alluring combination of emerald-green booths, exposed brick, distressed mirrors and spot lighting, The Third Man pays homage to Adolf Loos' legendary American Bar in Vienna, and Graham Greene's 1949 noir classic. The cocktails are evocative too, displaying the owners' culinary expertise and attention to detail. The Liquor on the Front is a fine example: a shaken, brightly hued mix of carrot and orange juices, gin, Cointreau and ginger. If you get peckish, order one of the bar's first-rate charcuterie and cheese plates. *116 Avenue C, T 212 598 1040, www.thethirdmannyc.com*

Red Rooster

Whatever the time of day, there's usually a buzz at Andrew Chapman and chef Marcus Samuelsson's restaurant, in the heart of Harlem. The personality of Ethiopian-born, Swedish-raised Samuelsson is reflected in the upbeat interior, which is lined with art by Gary Simmons, Sanford Biggers and Brandon Cox. The venue attracts a diverse crowd, whether it's to the dining room (opposite), the grocery (above) or the bar.

The menu is unique; order some dirty rice and shrimp, Helga's meatballs or crispy yardbird (fried chicken). On Sundays, brunch is a spirited (no-reservations) affair, with a gospel singer weaving amid diners. Downstairs, Ginny's Supper Club (T 212 421 3821) dishes up a fun blend of live music, cocktails and food.
310 Lenox Avenue, T 212 792 9001,
www.redroosterharlem.com

INSIDERS' GUIDE
ANISHKA CLARKE & NIYA BASCOM, INTERIOR DESIGNERS

Like myriad New Yorkers, Anishka Clarke (opposite, left) and Niya Bascom weren't born in the city, hailing from Jamaica and London, respectively. Happily settled in Lefferts Gardens, the co-owners of Ishka Designs create modern interiors for homes and restaurants. New York's diversity is what they both value most: 'I love Brooklyn's mix of cultures and architecture,' says Clarke.

Their day may begin with an organic breakfast at Tip of the Tongue (43 Lincoln Road, T 718 693 2253), while lunch is often a veggie bite at MOB (525 Atlantic Avenue, T 718 797 2555). Client meetings are often held over some barbecue and bourbon at Char No 4 (196 Smith Street, T 718 643 2106), or Jamaican food at Miss Lily's (132 W Houston Street, T 646 588 5375).

The duo receive their design fix at Michele Varian (27 Howard Street, T 212 343 0033), or From The Source (69 West Street, T 718 532 1671), which sells furniture constructed from salvaged wood. When it's time for a drink, Dick & Jane's Bar (266 Adelphi Street, T 347 227 8021) is a favourite, as is the Southern-fusion list at Soco (509 Myrtle Avenue, T 718 783 1936), which, according to Clarke, 'serves the very best mac 'n' cheese'. On the first Saturday of every month, the pair like to hang out at Reggae Retro at Littlefield (622 Degraw Street, T 718 930 1316), an old-school roots party where 'the vibe is authentic and the crowd laidback,' says Bascom.
For full addresses, see Resources.

ARCHITOUR

A GUIDE TO NEW YORK'S ICONIC BUILDINGS

Chicago is the birthplace of the skyscraper, Dubai boasts the tallest structure in the world, and Shanghai has more towers, but perhaps no city is as closely identified with the high-rise as New York. Money was the motivation to reach for the sky, but symbolism has always been immensely important here, from the automotive fantasies of Van Alen's art deco Chrysler Building (405 Lexington Avenue) to the soaring silhouette of One WTC (see p009). Indeed, it may be Gothamites' inordinate love of height that has enabled the city centre to retain its vibrancy, whereas so many of its American sister conurbations have become prisoners of suburban sprawl.

Structures such as Christian de Portzamparc's One57 (see p030), Gehry's 8 Spruce Street and Rafael Viñoly's 432 Park Avenue, which, at 425m, will be the tallest residential building in the Americas when it tops out in 2015, are all impressive. On the West Side, all eyes are on Hudson Yards. Previously a rail depot, its five hectares will encompass a mixed-use complex, green space and a subway extension in the first phase in 2018. Nearby, in the Meatpacking District, the Whitney Museum (see p032) relocates to its spacious new steel-clad home, designed by Renzo Piano, in 2015. Its former address, the 1966 Breuer Building (945 Madison Avenue) will host collaborative projects between the Whitney and the Metropolitan Museum of Art (1000 Fifth Avenue, T 212 535 7710).
For full addresses, see Resources.

New Museum

It isn't often that an art space has much in common with a rubbish bin. In actual fact, SANAA's New Museum of Contemporary Art, launched in 2007, may be the only building to be clad in the same wire mesh as its home city's trash receptacles. When the design – a series of piled-up silvery boxes – was revealed in 2003, it looked delightful yet impossible (not to mention improbable, given its location on the historically unsavoury Bowery). New York changes quickly, though, and what once seemed so unlikely (a fine-art museum on a street known for its homeless shelters) now makes sense. It didn't hurt that hip hotel The Bowery (see p016) opened nearby, or that, in 2013, the Hester Street Café took up residence on the ground floor. *235 Bowery, T 212 219 1222, www.newmuseum.org*

Lincoln Center

To celebrate its 50th anniversary, in 2010, the city's pre-eminent performing arts venue undertook a $1.2bn renovation programme. The aim was to unify the 6.5-hectare complex, creating new spaces and revamping existing buildings whose original architects included Eero Saarinen, Gordon Bunshaft and Philip Johnson. Diller Scofidio + Renfro and FXFOWLE tackled the overhaul of Alice Tully Hall, part of the 1969 Juilliard School, designed by Pietro Belluschi with Helge Westermann and Eduardo Catalano. The performance facilities have been modernised and a glass-walled foyer has been added to the theatre; the school boasts a transparent, cantilevered canopy, which bursts out of the building towards Broadway.
70 Lincoln Center Plaza, T 212 875 5000, www.lincolncenter.org

Seagram Building

Mies van der Rohe's 1958 masterpiece typified his less-is-more philosophy and is a triumph of the International Style. In fact, he stated this was his only work in the US that met his stringent European standards of design, borrowed from the architect's classic German Pavilion built for the 1929 Barcelona World's Fair. It was the first building to use floor-to-ceiling windows to achieve the modernist ideal of a curtain of glass, and although American construction codes prevented him from displaying the structural steel frame, Mies added non-supportive bronze-tinted beams. Despite the austere aesthetic, the extravagant use of materials meant this was the world's most expensive structure at the time. It served as a model for almost every NYC skyscraper that followed.

375 Park Avenue, www.375parkavenue.com

Morgan Library & Museum

Since JP Morgan Jr donated his father's personal library to the people of New York in 1924, it has to be said that not many of the great unwashed have felt the need to venture in. The collection of Gutenberg Bibles, manuscripts and paintings has always given off enough of an elitist whiff to scare the masses away. Renzo Piano's sublime 2006 expansion added an entrance on Madison Avenue, a glazed atrium and several galleries, increasing the exhibition space by more than 50 per cent – a design intended to beckon people in and pull together the three existing buildings. The Morgan has now become a destination museum and host to swanky, and lucrative, soirées. The old robber baron would have been pleased. *225 Madison Avenue, T 212 685 0008, www.themorgan.org*

FDR Four Freedoms Park

Louis Kahn was commissioned to create a memorial to FDR on Roosevelt Island in 1973. Working with landscape architect Harriet Pattison, Kahn conceived a simple design based on two quintessential forms: the room and the garden. He shaped a 'room' from large granite blocks, forming a serene space on the tip of the island. An extract from FDR's 1941 'Four Freedoms' speech is carved on one wall, opposite a 1933 bronze bust of the former president by sculptor Jo Davidson. Two paths lined with linden trees edge the triangular lawn. Kahn's death in 1974 and economic hitches delayed construction until 2010, and the park opened in 2012. Poised between Queens and Manhattan, it's a stunning site, accessible by cable car. Closed Tuesdays.
1 FDR Four Freedoms Park, Roosevelt Island, www.fdrfourfreedomspark.org

SHOPPING

THE BEST RETAIL THERAPY AND WHAT TO BUY

New York offers an abundance of seductive and diverse shopping opportunities, from the glossy boutiques lining Madison Avenue to the niche outlets dotted throughout Brooklyn. Matter (see p081), The Future Perfect (55 Great Jones Street, T 212 473 2500), R & Company (82 Franklin Street, T 212 343 7979) and BDDW (5 Crosby Street, T 212 625 1230) set a high standard for inspiring design, while the thoughtful selection of homewares sold at The Primary Essentials (opposite) also packs a punch. Another excellent option is the store helmed by renowned vintage and antiques collector Paula Rubenstein (21 Bond Street, T 212 966 8954). Having moved out of her Soho premises in 2012, she now runs an airy Noho shop full of Navajo textiles, glass cabinetry and industrial objects.

The 2013 launch of Dover Street Market (160 Lexington Avenue, T 646 837 7750) brought fresh energy (and hordes of fashionistas) to Murray Hill; like the original shop in London, the NYC store sells edgy, lesser-known labels alongside exclusive collaborations with the likes of Prada and Louis Vuitton. Cobbled Crosby Street continues to strengthen its reputation for interesting retail. Check out eyewear designer Mykita (No 109, T 212 343 9100), the cult menswear brand Carson Street Clothiers (No 63, T 212 925 2627), and the inaugural boutique of downtown darling Rachel Comey (No 95, T 212 334 0455), who opened here in 2014.

For full addresses, see Resources.

The Primary Essentials

An oasis of calm in the thick of Atlantic Avenue in Boerum Hill, Lauren Snyder's Brooklyn boutique sells design objects and artisanal curios from around the world. The former fashion stylist selects items that she feels marry style and function. You may spy Nambu Tekki ironware, Helen Levi's artful ceramics and EarthTuFace's natural skincare products. Snyder worked with her partner, architect Keith Burns, to customise the shop's interior, which is airy and uncluttered. Furnishings have been kept to a minimum – blue marble counter, and wooden display tables and cupboards. Keep an eye open for special commissions, such as the hand-dyed indigo blankets by Lookout & Wonderland, and Nicholas Newcomb's porcelain spoons.

372 Atlantic Avenue, T 718 522 1804, www.theprimaryessentials.com

David Weeks Studio
Best known for his hardwood Cubebots
and pliable animal figures, David Weeks
produces much more, as is clear on a
visit to his loft-like Tribeca showroom.
His creations include lighting, vivid rugs
and angular sofas, which are displayed
alongside collaborations with artists
such as wire sculptor Rodger Stevens.
Appointments recommended.
38 Walker Street, T 212 966 3433

Proenza Schouler

In 2012, Jack McCollough and Lazaro Hernandez took their downtown style, adored by art and fashion folk, uptown, with their first, flagship store. To carve out a suitably edgy emporium among Madison Avenue's tony storefronts, the couple enlisted their friend, Brit architect David Adjaye, who designed their Soho office. The two-level townhouse interior, a combination of glass, concrete, wood and steel, has a minimal aesthetic, which allows Proenza Schouler's distinctive designs to stand out. Adjaye worked the same magic on the brand's next branch, in Soho (T 212 420 7300). Another duplex, this larger shop presents its womenswear and accessories against marble walls and on poured-concrete pedestals.

822 Madison Avenue, T 212 585 3200, www.proenzaschouler.com

Creatures of Comfort

It's difficult to believe that Creatures of Comfort has been holding court in Nolita since 2010: the vitality that it brought to this popular shopping area is still palpable. An eclectic mix of products is presented across the sprawling 230 sq m exposed-brick store, overseen by buyer and owner Jade Lai, who started the company in Los Angeles in 2005. Lai lures customers with goods spanning Japanese furniture to Bernhard Willhelm nail varnish. Best of all, though, is the fashion on sale, specifically the womenswear. The company's own ready-to-wear label is complemented by Kenzo, Isabel Marant and Band of Outsiders, among others. There's also a project space located in the shop, which hosts pop-ups, exhibitions and events. *205 Mulberry Street, T 212 925 1005, www.creaturesofcomfort.us*

Hollander & Lexer
H&L's second Brooklyn boutique sells trend-resistant and vintage items: a sartorial formula that sealed the success of the first shop in Park Slope. Peruse the own-brand menswear and tight edit of accessories, such as Japanese scrubbing brushes. Owners Yaz Benmira and Brian Cousins designed the interior, which has a fabulous antique appearance.
103 Metropolitan Avenue, T 718 797 9117

Bottega Organica

Established by New York-based doctors, Bottega Organica's natural skincare line has been created using organic ingredients grown on the brand's own farm in Liguria, Italy. The products are infused with pure, cold-pressed olive oil from the region – a vitamin-rich, beneficial base for delivering optimal concentrations of essential oils, flower waters and extracts like camomile and sage. Rejuvenating face oils and serums, body formulas, soaps and hair mists are all displayed throughout the pared-down West Village boutique, which has an urban-rustic vibe thanks to the utilitarian furniture and reclaimed wood shelving. You can also buy herbal teas, extra-virgin olive oil and olives here, some harvested from the Ligurian farm.
117 Christopher Street, T 212 243 3537, www.bottegaorganica.com

Matter

Jamie Gray debuted his design emporium in Brooklyn's Park Slope in 2003, opening a Soho branch in 2007, which excels at presenting a pitch-perfect range of home accessories and furnishings. Gray, a Pratt Institute sculpture graduate, curates the in-house collection, MatterMade, which is sold next to brands such as the French company La Chance and London-based designer Michael Anastassiades. When seeking out collaborators, Gray places a strong emphasis on craftsmanship and artisanal skills, whether it be carpentry or glass-blowing. Among the American designs in store, look out for Bec Brittain's faceted lighting, the furniture of Ian Stell, and seating created by Roman and Williams under the MatterMade name. *405 Broome Street, T 212 343 2600, www.mattermatters.com*

Owen
Young retailer Phillip Salem is holding
his own in the saturated Meatpacking
District with his cult women's and men's
boutique, opened in 2012 in a former
gallery. The cool mix of contemporary
and emerging designers is perfectly
matched by Jeremy Barbour's interior
design – 25,000 brown paper sacks
meticulously stapled to the walls.
809 Washington Street, T 212 524 9770

RePOP

It didn't take long for vintage-design purveyor RePOP to outgrow its original store in Brooklyn's Clinton Hill. To meet the surge in demand for his wares, which he sources from across the US, owner Russell Boyle moved to a larger location in Williamsburg in 2012, a 148 sq m space in the same building as the Roebling Tea Room (T 718 963 0760). The showroom brims with items from various eras, and makes for inspiring browsing as a result. It's worth spending at least an hour or so here so you can scour the stock properly. Covetable finds on our visit ranged from antique dress dummies to original Danish Modern dressers and one-off lighting fixtures. RePOP's prices are fairer than you'll find in Manhattan, and bargaining isn't ruled out. Boyle also offers personal design consultations by appointment.
143 Roebling Street, T 718 260 8032, www.repopny.com

Cadet

This crisp Brooklyn boutique, which has an interior punctuated with ammunition belts, vintage globes and a portrait of a Civil War general, reinforces the military-inspired look for which menswear label Cadet has gained street cred. Although owners Raul Arevalo and Brad Schmidt appreciate the precise lines and timeless appeal of historic uniforms, they apply a modern spin to their clothes. Wardrobe basics such as button-down shirts and trousers are the most popular pieces, and customers take full advantage of the free alteration service. Everything is made at Cadet's Bushwick factory and sold only in its own stores; there are also branches in the East Village (T 646 633 4560) and Meatpacking District (T 917 722 2390).
46 N 6th Street, T 718 715 1695,
www.cadetusa.com

Alexander Wang

A luxe but relaxed aesthetic has rendered Alexander Wang's womenswear a fashion-pack staple. Opened in 2011, on Soho's grungy-glam Grand Street, the brand's Ryan Korban-conceived flagship store is a blend of boutique, gallery and design den. The large, all-white space boasts high ceilings, marble floors and a large steel cage that is used for seasonal installations. After browsing Wang's sexy, downtown-friendly clothing and accessories, head to the centre of the shop, where a lounge area beckons you to kick off your heels or, considering the environs, your Converse. The leather sofa and brass table laden with books and magazines should allay any retail fatigue, as will the fur hammock: simple but sumptuous, à la Wang.
103 Grand Street, T 212 977 9683, www.alexanderwang.com

SPORTS AND SPAS

WORK OUT, CHILL OUT OR JUST WATCH

From manicurists to masseurs, pedicurists to personal trainers, the Manhattanite has a small army of auxiliary support at his or her disposal, making this the ideal city for the beauty tourist. For a cut and colour, visit O&M (55 Little W 12th Street, T 212 255 2445), where old movies are silently projected on to the salon's walls. Nowhere pampers hands and feet better than Jin Soon Hand & Foot Spa (56 E 4th Street, T 212 473 2047), while the petite Savor Spa (327 W 11th Street, T 212 304 2887) uses its own line of organic products. The Shibui Spa (377 Greenwich Street, T 646 203 0045) at The Greenwich Hotel is hard to beat in terms of providing the full package, and not just because guests can swim under the roof of a rebuilt 250-year-old wood-and-bamboo Kyoto farmhouse. Yoga enthusiasts may want to try the high-energy classes at Lyons Den Power Yoga (279 Church Street, T 646 490 8888). Round off your beautifying regime with a conceptual scent from CB I Hate Perfume (318 Maujer Street, T 718 384 6890; Fridays and Saturdays).

If your sporting standpoint is more spectator than participant, catch the Knicks shooting hoops at Madison Square Garden (4 Pennsylvania Plaza, T 212 465 6741), or the Nets at the Barclays Center (620 Atlantic Avenue, T 917 618 6100); a baseball game at the Yankee Stadium (1 E 161st Street, T 718 293 4300); and US Open tennis at Flushing Meadows (Corona Park, T 718 760 6200). *For full addresses, see Resources.*

Cornelia Spa at The Surrey

There are plenty of luxurious spas in New York, but none that feel quite as discreet as this one. On the second floor of The Surrey hotel, Cornelia was designed by Lauren Rottet, who has done a fine job of carving out a chic relaxation area (above) and five well-appointed rooms within a tight space. Before your session, there are some thoughtful touches – a warm ginger-scented hand towel, a herbal neck pillow, a spoonful of artisanal honey, and a selection of delicate snacks, which are prepared by the spa's dedicated chef. Before you depart, you will be offered nibbles to complement your treatment. For the utmost privacy, there is no common changing area. Instead, each room comes equipped with a private armoire.

20 E 76th Street, T 646 358 3600, www.corneliaspaatthesurrey.com

Aqua

French expat Esther Gauthier brought
her native country's latest fitness craze to
Tribeca. Launched in 2013, Aqua spinning,
which involves underwater cycling, gives
a low-impact, high-resistance workout,
which, according to its devotees, reduces
stress on joints and tones up cellulite.
David Obuchowski, of DO Architecture,
joined forces with Gauthier to create
a studio that feels minimal and spa-like,

thanks to the blend of concrete, brick and
wood. The entrance area is a real success,
due to its oak flooring and contemporary
lighting; the darkwood changing rooms
have a monochromatic scheme. The pool
room is sparse yet bright, with white brick
walls and a lofty ceiling. All of Aqua's
spinning classes are single sex.
*78 Franklin Street, T 212 966 6784,
www.aquastudiony.com*

Hunter's Point South Park

Boosting the rejuvenation of Long Island City, a riverside district of Queens, this inspiring development was completed in 2013. Designed by Thomas Balsley Associates and Weiss/Manfredi, Hunter's Point comprises a sprawling oval-shaped green that accommodates all types of recreational activities, an urban beach that is prepped for picnickers and beach volleyballers, a garden in which native fauna is planted over freight rails, and an eye-catching pavilion next to the East River that contains a café and has an elevated wooden pier. Phase two will feature a 9m-high platform suspended over the water, all the better to catch that thrilling view of the Manhattan skyline; hire a bike and cycle here for a glimpse of new New York.

52-10 Center Boulevard

Rudy's Barbershop

For their first East Coast branch, located in a basement next to the Ace Hotel, the owners of Rudy's (Wade Weigel, David Petersen and the late Alex Calderwood) envisaged a salon with a unisex vibe. Aiming for a utilitarian but quirky feel, they began the process with Brooklyn-based WRK Design, sourcing fixtures from a former Remington Arms factory in Connecticut. They also scoured New York for items such as the baked enamel wall panels and vintage lighting, both found on the Bowery. A long outdoor bench and tiny private garden were added so you can socialise before and after your cut. Post-appointment, head upstairs to fragrance specialist Le Labo (T 212 532 7206), which opened a branch next door in 2013.
14 W 29th Street, T 212 532 7200,
www.rudysbarbershop.com

ESCAPES

WHERE TO GO IF YOU WANT TO LEAVE TOWN

Gothamites claim that when you leave New York, you ain't going nowhere – although in summer, the city's border seems to stretch to include the length of Long Island. When the going gets hot, the hot crowd gets going. (If you can stand the humidity in town, your reward will be blissfully empty shops and restaurants.) Escape options are many, whether your taste is for an art expedition (see p098), surfing off Montauk – stay at The Surf Lodge (183 Edgemere Street, T 631 483 5037) or Ruschmeyer's (161 Second House Road, T 631 668 2877) – or hiking in the Catskills. Upstate, the cheekily named Stickett Inn (3380 Route 97, Barryville, T 845 557 0913) offers four modern suites and a log cabin. Situated by the scenic Delaware River, it's a two-hour drive from the city.

If you visit the Hamptons, make sure you have a friend with a house, or rent a place far in advance. To avoid bumper-to-bumper traffic, get there on the Cannonball train on the Long Island Rail Road, or the Hampton Jitney (www.hamptonjitney.com), whose glamorous passengers give new meaning to coach travel. Shelter Island is less intense; go by ferry and stay at André Balazs' Sunset Beach hotel (35 Shore Road, T 631 749 2001). Closer to the city, book one of the 12 artist-designed rooms at Playland Motel (97-20 Rockaway Beach Boulevard, T 347 954 9063), a hip hotel with a lively bar, just a block away from the locals' surf spot of choice. *For full addresses, see Resources.*

Topping Rose House, Bridgehampton
Relaunched in its present guise in spring 2013, Simon Critchell and Bill Campbell's Topping Rose House manages to convey a sense of history while fully embracing contemporary design. The property was subject to a dramatic three-year overhaul that saw Roger Ferris + Partners carefully restore the original 1842 house and barn, and add a brand-new building and modern cottages (all of which cater for guests), as well as a spa and event space. Another major attraction is the hotel's top-notch restaurant, helmed by lauded chef Tom Colicchio. The seasonal American menu makes the most of locally grown produce, including vegetables, fruit and herbs harvested from the hotel's own farm. *One Bridgehampton, Sag Harbor Turnpike, Bridgehampton, T 631 537 0870, www.toppingrosehouse.com*

Parrish Art Museum, Long Island

Artists have populated Long Island's East End since the late 19th century, when commuting from New York was made easier by an extension of the Long Island Rail Road. Notable figures have been drawn by the light and the beauty of the landscape, from Impressionist William Merritt Chase to abstract expressionists Jackson Pollock and Willem de Kooning. The Parrish Art Museum was founded in Southampton in 1898, by collector Samuel Longstreth Parrish. In 2012, it moved into a new building by Herzog & de Meuron. Modelled on an East End artist's studio, and featuring two striking overhangs, the sky-lit space has tripled the exhibition area for the permanent collection of early 19th-century to present-day East End art.
279 Montauk Highway, Water Mill,
T 631 283 2118, www.parrishart.org

Richard Meier Model Museum
If you're looking for a reason to venture over the Hudson, Richard Meier's Model Museum is a good one. Located in the Mana Contemporary art complex, it displays more than 400 handmade architectural models created during the architect's 50-year career. One of the most notable is an 11m-long model of the Getty Center in LA, made entirely from wood. An archive of small-scale sketches, photographs and renderings is exhibited across floor-to-ceiling shelves. Intended as a resource for both visitors and students, the museum also houses Meier's research library and displays some of his artwork. His daughter, Ana Meier, has a furniture showroom next door. Visits are by appointment only. *Mana Contemporary, 888 Newark Avenue, Jersey City, T 212 967 6060*

Glass House, New Canaan
The Connecticut town of New Canaan,
about 40 miles north-east of NYC, boasts
some of the finest examples of modern
American architecture. The most famous
is Philip Johnson's home, the Glass House
(pictured), completed in 1949. It is perhaps
the purest expression of the International
Style. Tours must be booked in advance.
*Visitor Center, 199 Elm Street,
T 866 811 4111, www.theglasshouse.org*

NOTES
SKETCHES AND MEMOS

RESOURCES
CITY GUIDE DIRECTORY

HOTELS
ADDRESSES AND ROOM RATES

Hôtel Americano 026
Room rates:
double, from $255;
Studio Suite, from $455
518 W 27th Street
T 212 216 0000
www.hotel-americano.com

Andaz Wall Street 024
Room rates:
double, from $285;
Room 1513, from $285
75 Wall Street
T 212 590 1234
www.andaz.com

The Bowery Hotel 016
Room rates:
double, from $375
335 Bowery
T 212 505 9100
www.theboweryhotel.com

The Broome 017
Room rastes:
double, from $400;
Penthouse, from $700
431 Broome Street
T 212 431 2929
www.thebroomenyc.com

The Chatwal 023
Room rates:
double, from $925;
Producer Suite, from $2,825
130 W 44th Street
T 212 764 6200
www.thechatwalny.com

Crosby Street Hotel 025
Room rates:
double, from $595;
One Bedroom Suite, from $2,500
79 Crosby Street
T 212 226 6400
www.firmdalehotels.com

Four Seasons 022
Room rates:
double, from $795;
Ty Warner Penthouse, $45,000
57 E 57th Street
T 212 758 5700
www.fourseasons.com/newyork

The High Line Hotel 016
Room rates:
double, from $535
180 Tenth Avenue
T 212 929 3888
www.thehighlinehotel.com

Hotel Hugo 016
Room rates:
double, from $400
525 Greenwich Street
T 888 335 8944
www.hotelhugony.com

The Jane 016
Room rates:
double, from $345
113 Jane Street
T 212 924 6700
www.thejanenyc.com

Loews Regency 016
Room rates:
double, from $570
540 Park Avenue
T 212 759 4100
www.loewshotels.com/regency-hotel

The Ludlow 016
Room rates:
double, from $305
180 Ludlow Street
T 212 432 1818
www.theludlownyc.com

The Marlton 018
Room rates:
double, from $250;
Queen Deluxe, from $300
5 W 8th Street
T 212 321 0100
www.marltonhotel.com

The Nolitan 027
Room rates:
double, from $290
30 Kenmare Street
T 212 925 2555
www.nolitanhotel.com

The NoMad Hotel 031
Room rates:
double, from $425;
Grande Room, from $535;
Suite, from $750
1170 Broadway
T 212 796 1500
www.thenomadhotel.com

Park Hyatt 030
Room rates:
double, from $1,295
One57
153 W 57th Street
T 646 774 1234
www.newyork.park.hyatt.com

Playland Motel 096
Room rates:
double, from $95
97-20 Rockaway Beach Boulevard
Rockaway Beach
T 347 954 9063
www.playlandmotel.com

Quin 016
Room rates:
double, from $500
101 W 57th Street
T 212 245 7846
www.thequinhotel.com

Ruschmeyer's 096
Room rates:
double, from $480
161 Second House Road
Montauk
Long Island
T 631 668 2877
www.kingandgrove.com

The Standard East Village 028
Room rates:
double, from $395;
Noho Studio, from $645
25 Cooper Square
T 212 475 5700
www.standardhotels.com/east-village

The Stickett Inn 096
Room rates:
double, from $120
3380 Route 97
Barryville
T 845 557 0913
www.stickettinn.com

Sunset Beach 096
Room rates:
double, from $480
35 Shore Road
Shelter Island
Long Island
T 631 749 2001
www.sunsetbeachli.com

The Surf Lodge 096
Room rates:
double, from $550
183 Edgemere Street
Montauk
Long Island
T 631 483 5037
www.thesurflodge.com

Topping Rose House 097
Room rates:
double, from $525
One Bridgehampton
Sag Harbor Turnpike
Bridgehampton
Long Island
T 631 537 0870
www.toppingrosehouse.com

Viceroy 016
Room rates:
double, from $355
124 W 57th Street
T 212 830 8000
www.viceroyhotelsandresorts.com

Wythe Hotel 020
Room rates:
double, from $300;
Manhattan View King Room, from $450
80 Wythe Avenue
Brooklyn
T 718 460 8000
www.wythehotel.com

WALLPAPER* CITY GUIDES

Executive Editor
Rachael Moloney

Editor
Ella Marshall

Authors
Katie Chang
Pei-Ru Keh

Art Editor
Eriko Shimazaki
Original Design
Loran Stosskopf
Map Illustrator
Russell Bell

Photography Editor
Elisa Merlo
Assistant Photography Editor
Nabil Butt

Production Manager
Vanessa Todd-Holmes

Chief Sub-Editor
Nick Mee
Sub-Editor
Farah Shafiq

Editorial Assistant
Emilee Jane Tombs

Contributor
David Kaufman

Interns
Ayaka Nakamura
Victoria Purcell
Rosemary Stopher

Wallpaper* ® is a
registered trademark
of IPC Media Limited

First published 2006
Revised and updated
2008, 2009, 2010, 2011,
2013 and 2014

© Phaidon Press Limited

All prices are correct at
the time of going to press,
but are subject to change.

Printed in China

Phaidon Press Limited
Regent's Wharf
All Saints Street
London N1 9PA

Phaidon Press Inc
65 Bleecker Street
New York, NY 10012

Phaidon® is a registered
trademark of Phaidon
Press Limited

www.phaidon.com

A CIP Catalogue record for
this book is available from
the British Library.

ISBN 978 0 7148 6835 6

PHOTOGRAPHERS

Iwan Baan
High Line, p037

Magda Biernat
Hôtel Americano, p026
Red Rooster, p060, p061
Lincoln Center, pp066-067
Hollander & Lexer,
pp078-079
Matter, p081
Rudy's Barbershop,
pp094-095

Ron Blunt
Glass House, pp102-103

Roger Casas
Hearst Tower, p013
Austrian Cultural
Forum, p014
Woolworth Building, p015
Seagram Building, p068

Baldomero Fernandez
The Chatwal, p023
Creatures of Comfort, p077

Floto+Warner Studio
The Nolitan, p027

Hotel Existence
Andaz Wall Street, p024

Noah Kalina
Momofuku Ssäm Bar, p055

Dean Kaufman
New Museum, p065

Fran Parente
New York city view,
inside front cover
9/11 Memorial, pp010-011
The Broome, p017
The Marlton, p018, p019
The Standard East
Village, pp028-029
Park Hyatt, p030
The Apartment by
The Line, pp034-035
All'Onda, pp038-039
Tørst, p041
The Monarch
Room, pp042-043
Narcissa, p044, p045
Runner & Stone, p046
Potlikker, p047
Pearl & Ash, pp048-049
Atera, p050
Wallflower, p051
Alder, pp052-053
Antica Pesa, p054
Toro, pp056-057
Sushi Nakazawa, p058
The Third Man, p059
Anishka Clarke and
Niya Bascom, p063
The Primary
Essentials, p073
David Weeks
Studio, pp074-075
Proenza Schouler, p076
RePOP, pp084-085
Cadet, p086
Cornelia Spa at
The Surrey, p089
Aqua, pp090-091

Hunter's Point South
Park, pp092-093

Gianni Pipoli
Bottega Organica, p080

Matthu Placek
Parrish Art Museum,
pp098-099

Mark Rose
Topping Rose House, p097

Annie Schlechter
Four Seasons, p022

Jason Schmidt
David Zwirner, p033

Steven Sze
Richard Meier Model
Museum, pp100-101

Paul Warchol
FDR Four Freedoms
Park, pp070-071

**Courtesy of The
NoMad Hotel**
The NoMad Hotel, p031

Courtesy of Wythe Hotel
Wythe Hotel, pp020-021

**© Judd Foundation/VAGA,
NY/DACS, London 2014**
101 Spring Street, p036

NEW YORK
A COLOUR-CODED GUIDE TO THE HOT 'HOODS

TRIBECA/THE BATTERY
Lower Manhattan embraces Wall Street and, to the north, hip shops and restaurants

UPPER WEST SIDE
This is Woody Allen territory, characterised by the apartment blocks of the bourgeoisie

WEST VILLAGE
A charming district, full of tree-lined avenues, and plenty of chichi boutiques and cafés

SOHO
Big fashion brands attract tourists, but there are interesting galleries in the area too

UPPER EAST SIDE
Visit the swanky stores on Madison Avenue and some of the best museums in the world

MIDTOWN
The throbbing business heart of New York is the location of the neon-tastic Times Square

CHELSEA
New York's power art crowd gather day and night in this slick West Side neighbourhood

EAST VILLAGE/LOWER EAST SIDE
Cool bars, shops and cultural spaces pepper this increasingly wealthy part of town

For a full description of each neighbourhood, see the Introduction.
Featured venues are colour-coded, according to the district in which they are located.